UNVEILING THE VEIL TWO NATION: ISRAEL AND PALESTINE

First edition. December 23, 2024.

ISBN: 979-8230058465

Written by Dans Hardyans.

"Behind every border lies a story, behind every conflict, a shared humanity. The journey to peace between Israel and Palestine begins not with dominance, but with understanding and compassion."

"When a land cries for justice and its people bleed for recognition, humanity must rise above divisions. The story of Israel and Palestine is not about choosing sides, but about reclaiming the dignity of every soul."

Unveiling The Veil Two Nation: Israel and Palestine

Introduction

The story of Israel and Palestine is one of the most complex and emotionally charged conflicts in modern history. To understand the roots of this ongoing struggle, it is essential to delve deeply into the history of the Jewish people, as told in sacred scriptures, and to examine their tumultuous journey through centuries of exile, persecution, and eventual establishment in Palestine.

This book explores the journey of the Jewish people from their origins as "Bani Israel" in the scriptures, their relationships with prophets, and their struggles with faith, to their exile from Europe, and the creation of the state of Israel in the 20th century. It also sheds light on the Palestinian experience, a people displaced, oppressed, and fighting for their homeland amidst the geopolitical complexities of the modern era.

Through sacred texts, historical narratives, and the lens of human resilience, this book seeks to provide a balanced account of the conflict. It does not aim to justify or condemn but to illuminate the shared and contested histories of two nations.

Chapter 1. The Jewish People in Sacred Scriptures

The Story of Bani Israel

The Jewish people, referred to as "Bani Israel" in Islamic scripture and "Israelites" in the Bible, hold a significant role in the Abrahamic faiths. Their journey begins with the covenant between God and Abraham (Ibrahim), a central figure in Judaism, Christianity, and Islam. This covenant promised that Abraham's descendants would inherit the land of Canaan, provided they remained faithful to God (Genesis 15:18–21, Quran 2:124).

From Abraham's lineage through Isaac (Ishaq) and Jacob (Ya'qub), also known as Israel, the Children of Israel emerged as recipients of divine laws and guidance. However, their relationship with God, as described in the Torah, Bible, and Quran, was marked by both devotion and rebellion.

The Exodus and Covenant at Sinai

According to the Torah (Book of Exodus), the Israelites were enslaved in Egypt until God delivered them through Moses (Musa). The parting of the Red Sea and the giving of the Ten Commandments at Mount Sinai became defining moments of their faith.

However, the Israelites' subsequent actions often betrayed their covenant. In the Torah, it is written:

> "They have been quick to turn away from what I commanded them and have made themselves an idol cast in the

shape of a calf. They have bowed down to it and sacrificed to it." (Exodus 32:8)

The Quran mirrors this account:

> "And [recall] when We took your covenant and raised over you the mount, [saying], 'Take what We have given you with determination.'... Then you turned away after that. And if not for the favor of Allah upon you and His mercy, you would have been among the losers." (Quran 2:63-64)

Wandering in the Desert

Both the Torah and the Quran recount how the Israelites refused to enter the Promised Land out of fear, leading to their punishment of wandering in the wilderness for 40 years (Numbers 14:26–35, Quran 5:20–26).

A Cycle of Faith and Betrayal

Both the Bible and the Quran highlight the recurring cycle of divine blessings, rebellion, and punishment faced by the Israelites. Their repeated disobedience led to invasions, exile, and suffering, as seen in the destruction of the First and Second Temples and their captivity in Babylon.

Prophecies of Exile and Return

The Book of Deuteronomy warns of exile as a consequence of disobedience:

> "The Lord will scatter you among all nations, from one end of the earth to the other. There you will worship other gods—gods of wood and stone, which neither you nor your ancestors have known." (Deuteronomy 28:64)

Yet, these scriptures also promise eventual restoration if they repent:

> "Then the Lord your God will restore your fortunes and have compassion on you and gather you again from all the nations where he scattered you." (Deuteronomy 30:3)

The Covenant with God

The story of the Jewish people begins with Abraham (Ibrahim), who entered into a sacred covenant with God.

The Promise of Canaan: God promised Abraham that his descendants would inherit the land of Canaan if they remained faithful to Him (Genesis 15:18–21; Quran 2:124).

The Test of Faith: Abraham's willingness to sacrifice his son, an act commanded by God, is a cornerstone of the covenant. While Jewish and Christian traditions name Isaac, Islamic tradition identifies Ishmael as the son involved.

Lessons: The covenant highlighted the importance of faith and obedience as conditions for divine favor.

The Exodus and the Covenant at Sinai

The Israelites' enslavement in Egypt and their subsequent liberation under Moses (Musa) is one of the most dramatic narratives in sacred history.

The Liberation: The parting of the Red Sea, as described in the Book of Exodus and the Quran, marked their miraculous escape from Pharaoh's oppression (Exodus 14:21–22; Quran 26:63).

The Ten Commandments: At Mount Sinai, God gave Moses the Ten Commandments, laws meant to guide the Israelites in righteousness (Exodus 20:1–17; Quran 7:145).

Acts of Rebellion: Despite these blessings, the Israelites repeatedly disobeyed God:

1. The Golden Calf: While Moses was on Mount Sinai, the Israelites crafted a golden calf and worshipped it, betraying their covenant with God (Exodus 32:8; Quran 2:51).

Quran: "And Moses said to his people, 'O my people, you have wronged yourselves by taking the calf [for worship]. So repent to your Creator.'" (Quran 2:54).

2. Complaints in the Wilderness: The Israelites complained about their hardships and longed to return to Egypt, doubting God's provision (Numbers 14:2–4; Quran 2:61).

Divine Punishment: For their rebellion and lack of faith, the Israelites were condemned to wander the wilderness for 40 years (Numbers 14:33–34; Quran 5:26).

The Rejection of Prophets

Throughout their history, the Israelites were blessed with prophets sent by God to guide them. Yet, many of these prophets faced rejection, persecution, and even death.

The Killing of Prophets: Both the Bible and Quran lament the Israelites' treatment of God's messengers.

Bible: "Jerusalem, Jerusalem, you who kill the prophets and stone those sent to you..." (Matthew 23:37).

Quran: "And We gave Moses the Scripture and followed up after him with messengers. And We gave Jesus, the son of Mary, clear proofs and supported him with the Holy Spirit. But is it [not] that every time a messenger came to you, [O Children of Israel], with what your souls did not desire, you were arrogant? And a party [of messengers] you denied and another party you killed." (Quran 2:87).

Examples of Rejected Prophets:

1. Moses (Musa): Despite leading them out of Egypt, Moses faced constant defiance and complaints.

2. Elijah (Eliyahu): In the Bible, Elijah fled for his life after opposing Israelite rulers who worshipped Baal (1 Kings 19:1–3).

3. Jesus (Isa): The New Testament and Quran describe how Jesus was rejected by many Israelites, despite performing miracles (John 1:11; Quran 5:110).

Betrayals and Punishments

The Israelites' betrayals often resulted in divine punishment, reinforcing the consequences of disobedience.

The Kingdoms of Israel and Judah: After the golden age under David and Solomon, the united kingdom split, leading to moral corruption and idolatry.

The northern kingdom of Israel was conquered by the Assyrians in 722 BCE.

The southern kingdom of Judah fell to the Babylonians in 586 BCE, resulting in the destruction of the First Temple and exile to Babylon.

Bible: "Because they have forsaken Me and burned incense to other gods... My anger will burn against this place and will not be quenched." (2 Kings 22:17).

Altering Sacred Scriptures: The Quran accuses some Israelites of distorting God's words for their own gain:

Quran: "So woe to those who write the 'scripture' with their own hands, then say, 'This is from Allah,' to exchange it for a small price." (Quran 2:79).

Conclusion: A People Blessed Yet Rebellious

The sacred scriptures portray the Jewish people as recipients of unparalleled blessings from God, including divine guidance, miracles, and prophets. However, these narratives also highlight a recurring pattern of betrayal and rebellion:

Faith and Disobedience: Their history reflects a cycle of faithfulness followed by disobedience, leading to punishment and exile.

Rejection of Prophets: Despite being chosen to uphold God's laws, their rejection of prophets and divine guidance often led to their downfall.

A Testament to Human Nature: The Israelites' story is a microcosm of humanity's struggle with faith, temptation, and redemption.

Reflection: While these narratives emphasize the Israelites' transgressions, they also serve as lessons for all humanity, underscoring the importance of faith, gratitude, and obedience to divine will. Their resilience as a people, despite repeated trials and punishments, also highlights the enduring power of faith and identity.

This deeper understanding of their sacred history sets the stage for comprehending the complexities of their modern struggles and interactions with others in the region.

Israel: A Small Nation with a Great Story

Historically, the Israelites were a small, tribal people. They were not a powerful empire like Egypt, Babylon, or Assyria, but a pastoral and agricultural community living in a narrow strip of land between the Jordan River and the Mediterranean Sea. This land, often referred to as the Land of Canaan or the Promised Land, was strategically located at the crossroads of major civilizations, making it both a blessing and a curse for the Israelites.

A Small Nation in a Great Land

The Bible and the Quran emphasize the modest size of Israel and its dependence on divine protection.

In the Torah

> "The Lord did not set His love on you nor choose you because you were more in number than any other people, for you were the least of all peoples." (Deuteronomy 7:7)

This verse highlights the Israelites' reliance on God's favor, rather than their own strength, to survive and thrive amidst larger and more powerful neighbors.

In the Quran

> "And We caused the people who had been oppressed to inherit the eastern regions of the land and the western ones, which We had blessed." (Quran 7:137)

This reflects their modest beginnings as an oppressed people who were later given a land of their own.

Their Early Kingdoms

The establishment of the united monarchy under Saul, David, and Solomon was the golden age of Israelite history. David expanded their territory and established Jerusalem as the political and religious center, while Solomon built the First Temple.

However, their glory was short-lived. The kingdom split into two—the northern kingdom of Israel and the southern kingdom of Judah. This division weakened them, making them vulnerable to external invasions.

The Fall of Israel

In 722 BCE, the Assyrian Empire conquered the northern kingdom, leading to the dispersion of the "Ten Lost Tribes."

The Fall of Judah

In 586 BCE, the Babylonian Empire destroyed the southern kingdom, including the First Temple, and exiled the population to Babylon.

A People of Covenant, Not Power

Unlike powerful empires that relied on military might and wealth, the Israelites' strength lay in their covenant with God and their spiritual resilience. Their scriptures, culture, and laws allowed them to survive as a people even after losing their land and political independence.

> "Not by might nor by power, but by My Spirit," says the Lord Almighty. (Zechariah 4:6)

This verse encapsulates the essence of Israel's identity—a small nation with a spiritual mission, rather than a global empire.

From Obscurity to Global Attention

Despite their modest beginnings, the Israelites' story has had a profound impact on the world. Judaism laid the foundation for Christianity and Islam, two of the world's largest religions. Their scriptures, laws, and moral teachings have shaped Western civilization and continue to influence billions of people.

In the ancient world, they were one of many small tribes.

In the medieval era, they were a scattered and persecuted minority.

In the modern era, they are the focus of intense political, religious, and cultural debate.

The Shift to Modern Israel

While ancient Israel was a small kingdom with limited influence, the modern state of Israel, established in 1948, has become a major player in global politics. This transformation is a result of historical events, including the diaspora, the Holocaust, and the Zionist movement.

Chapter 2: The Expulsion of the Jews – A History of Persecution and Displacement

The Jewish people, despite their historical and religious significance, have faced waves of expulsion, persecution, and displacement throughout history. This chapter delves into the key events and reasons behind their expulsion from various countries, shedding light on the socio-political and religious factors that drove these actions.

The Early Expulsions in Antiquity

Babylonian Exile (586 BCE):

After the destruction of the First Temple by the Babylonian king Nebuchadnezzar, the Jewish population of Judah was exiled to Babylon. This marked the first major displacement of the Jewish people, forcing them to adapt to life in a foreign land while maintaining their religious identity.

Roman Expulsions (70 CE and 135 CE):

Following the destruction of the Second Temple in 70 CE, the Romans expelled the Jewish population from Jerusalem. The Bar Kokhba Revolt in 135 CE resulted in another large-scale expulsion, with Jews forbidden to live in Jerusalem. These expulsions scattered the Jewish people across the Roman Empire.

Expulsions in Medieval Europe

The Middle Ages were marked by widespread anti-Semitism, fueled by religious intolerance, economic jealousy, and scapegoating of the Jewish community for various crises.

England (1290):

King Edward I issued the Edict of Expulsion, banishing all Jews from England. This was largely due to accusations of usury, where Jews were blamed for exploiting Christians through moneylending. The expulsion lasted for over 350 years until Jews were readmitted under Oliver Cromwell in the 1650s.

France (1306, 1322, and 1394):

Jews were expelled multiple times from France during the reigns of Philip IV, Charles IV, and Charles VI. Economic motives played a significant role, as rulers sought to confiscate Jewish property and cancel debts owed to Jewish moneylenders.

Spain (1492):

One of the most infamous expulsions occurred under Ferdinand and Isabella, who issued the Alhambra Decree. Jews were forced to convert to Christianity or leave Spain. Many who converted (Conversos) were later persecuted by the Spanish Inquisition for allegedly practicing Judaism in secret.

Portugal (1496):

Inspired by Spain, King Manuel I of Portugal expelled the Jews, forcing many to convert. Those who refused to leave or convert faced brutal persecution.

Expulsions in Eastern Europe

Eastern Europe, while initially more tolerant, eventually followed similar patterns of persecution.

Germany (1350s–1500s):

Waves of expulsions occurred during the Black Death, as Jews were falsely accused of poisoning wells. Cities like Cologne, Nuremberg, and Augsburg expelled their Jewish populations.

Poland and Russia (17th–19th centuries):

Although Poland was initially a refuge for Jews, expulsions began as political and economic tensions rose. In Russia, pogroms and expulsions intensified under the Tsars, particularly in the Pale of Settlement.

The Role of Religious and Economic Factors

Religious Intolerance:

The Catholic Church and later Protestant movements often portrayed Jews as Christ-killers and heretics, fueling hostility. Many of these accusations were unfounded but deeply ingrained in European society.

Economic Jealousy:

Jews were often restricted to certain professions, such as moneylending and trade, leading to resentment from the Christian majority. Rulers frequently expelled Jews to confiscate their wealth or cancel debts owed to them.

The Diaspora and the Search for Refuge

With each expulsion, the Jewish community sought refuge in more tolerant regions.

The Ottoman Empire (15th–16th centuries):

After the expulsion from Spain and Portugal, many Jews found refuge in the Ottoman Empire, where they were welcomed by Sultan Bayezid II. Cities like Istanbul, Thessaloniki, and Izmir became centers of Sephardic Jewish life.

Netherlands (16th–17th centuries):

The Netherlands emerged as a haven for Jews fleeing persecution in Spain and Portugal. Amsterdam, in particular, became a thriving Jewish community.

The Journey to Palestine

While many Jews sought refuge in tolerant regions, some dreamed of returning to their ancestral homeland in Palestine. Small communities of Jews continued to live in the Holy Land, but the idea of mass migration only gained momentum in the 19th century with the rise of Zionism.

> Reflection:

The repeated expulsions and persecutions forged a resilient Jewish identity, deeply rooted in religion and culture. However, these historical traumas also planted the seeds of future conflicts, as the displaced Jewish populations sought a permanent homeland.

Rebellion and Consequences in Sacred Texts

The expulsions and sufferings of the Jewish people can be viewed as outcomes of their repeated defiance of divine commands, as detailed in sacred texts.

From the Bible:

The Book of Judges illustrates the Israelites' cyclical rebellion:

> "They abandoned the Lord, the God of their ancestors, who had brought them out of Egypt. They followed and worshiped various gods of the peoples around them. They aroused the Lord's anger." (Judges 2:12)

This disobedience often resulted in divine punishment, including invasions by foreign powers.

> "I will scatter you among the nations and will draw out my sword and pursue you. Your land will be laid waste, and your cities will lie in ruins." (Leviticus 26:33)

From the Quran:

The Quran describes how the Israelites repeatedly broke covenants:

> "And when We took your covenant and raised over you the mount, [saying], 'Take what We have given you with determination.' Then you turned away after that. And if not for the favor of Allah upon you and His mercy, you would have been among the losers." (Quran 2:63-64)

Reflection:

Sacred texts emphasize that the Israelites' repeated disobedience and arrogance brought about divine retribution, including exile and hardship.

Patterns of Defiance and Punishment

The Golden Calf Incident:

A recurring theme in the scriptures is the Israelites' tendency to stray from faith even after witnessing divine miracles.

Bible: "They have been quick to turn away from what I commanded them and have made themselves an idol cast in the shape of a calf. They have bowed down to it and sacrificed to it." (Exodus 32:8)

Quran: "And [recall] when Moses said to his people, 'O my people, indeed you have wronged yourselves by your taking of the calf [for worship].'" (Quran 2:54)

The Refusal to Enter the Promised Land:

Their refusal to trust God's promise of the land of Canaan led to further punishment:

Bible: "Not one of you will enter the land I swore with uplifted hand to make your home, except Caleb son of Jephunneh and Joshua son of Nun." (Numbers 14:30)

Quran: "They said, 'O Moses, indeed within it is a people of tyrannical strength, and indeed, we will never enter it until they leave it; but if they leave it, then we will enter.'" (Quran 5:22)

Exile as a Consequence of Betrayal:

The Israelites' continued defiance culminated in the destruction of their temples and exile:

Bible: "Therefore the Lord was very angry with Israel and removed them from his presence. Only the tribe of Judah was left." (2 Kings 17:18)

Quran: "So when the time came for the second of the warnings, We sent your enemies to sadden your faces and to enter the temple in Jerusalem, as they entered it the first time, and to destroy what they had taken over with [total] destruction." (Quran 17:7)

Historical Expulsions as a Reflection of Scriptural Narratives

The historical expulsions of the Jewish people echo the patterns described in sacred texts:

Babylonian Exile (586 BCE): A consequence of moral corruption and idolatry as described in the Book of Jeremiah:

> "The people of Judah have done evil in my eyes, declares the Lord. They have set up their detestable idols in the house that bears my Name and have defiled it." (Jeremiah 7:30)

Roman Expulsions (70 CE and 135 CE): The refusal to accept Roman authority and subsequent revolts led to catastrophic consequences, fulfilling biblical warnings of scattering:

> "The Lord will scatter you among all nations, from one end of the earth to the other." (Deuteronomy 28:64)

Moral Lessons from Rebellion and Expulsion

Recurring Theme: The sacred texts and historical accounts highlight a pattern of divine patience followed by judgment when the covenant is broken.

Bible: "Because of our sins and the sins of our ancestors, Jerusalem and your people have become the talk of all those around us." (Daniel 9:16)

Quran: "But because of their breaking their covenant, We cursed them and made their hearts hard. They distort words from their [proper] usages and have forgotten a portion of that of which they were reminded." (Quran 5:13)

Reflection: These events serve as lessons not only for the Jewish people but for all humanity about the consequences of defiance and the importance of faithfulness to divine guidance.

Conclusion

The repeated expulsions and persecutions faced by the Jewish people are not merely results of external hostility but also reflect their historical disobedience and betrayal of divine commands. Sacred texts emphasize their privileged status as a chosen people, yet their defiance, arrogance, and ingratitude often led to divine punishment and suffering.

The pattern of rebellion and exile is a reminder of the dangers of forgetting one's obligations to God and society. While their resilience is notable, their history also serves as a cautionary tale of the consequences of moral and spiritual failure.

This deeper exploration reinforces the notion that the Jewish people's history, as portrayed in both scriptures and historical events, reflects a cycle of divine blessings, human arrogance, and eventual punishment—a narrative that holds lessons for all nations and peoples.

Chapter 3: The Flight to Palestine – The Path to a Homeland

The Rising Tide of Anti-Semitism in Europe

By the 19th century, anti-Semitism in Europe had taken new forms. While traditional religious hatred persisted, secular ideologies now painted Jews as economic parasites or political threats. This created an increasingly hostile environment:

The Pogroms in Eastern Europe:

From the late 1800s, Jews in the Russian Empire faced waves of pogroms—violent, state-sanctioned attacks on Jewish communities. The most infamous pogroms occurred between 1881 and 1884, following the assassination of Tsar Alexander II, for which Jews were falsely blamed. Hundreds of communities were destroyed, prompting mass emigration.

The Dreyfus Affair (France, 1894):

The wrongful conviction of Captain Alfred Dreyfus, a Jewish officer in the French army, highlighted the deep-rooted anti-Semitism in Western Europe. This incident convinced many Jews that assimilation was not the answer to their plight.

The Lives of Jews in the Diaspora Before Migration

Before their migration to Palestine, the Jewish communities in Europe faced widespread discrimination, violence, and exclusion, creating a sense of urgency for a national homeland.

Eastern Europe and Russia:

In the late 19th and early 20th centuries, pogroms in the Russian Empire devastated Jewish communities. These violent state-sanctioned attacks resulted in the destruction of property, loss of life, and mass displacement.

Jewish communities in Poland and Eastern Europe, though initially welcomed, eventually faced restrictive laws and economic exploitation.

Western Europe:

Even in relatively progressive countries like France, anti-Semitism persisted, as evidenced by the Dreyfus Affair (1894), where a Jewish military officer was falsely accused of treason.

The rise of nationalism and racial theories in Europe further marginalized Jewish populations, fueling the need for a safe haven.

As the centuries unfolded, the Jewish diaspora continued to search for a safe haven. Persecution and expulsions had left their mark, and by the late 19th century, a growing sense of urgency emerged among Jewish communities worldwide. This chapter explores the factors that led to the Jewish migration to Palestine, including the impact of anti-Semitism, the rise of Zionism, and the geopolitical shifts that shaped their journey.

Religious and Secular Motivations in Zionism

The Zionist movement was not monolithic; it was shaped by diverse ideologies that reflected the varied aspirations of the Jewish people.

Secular Zionism:

Led by Theodor Herzl and other intellectuals, secular Zionists envisioned a modern, independent state for Jews, free from persecution. Herzl's Der Judenstaat (The Jewish State) became the manifesto for political Zionism.

Religious Zionism:

Many Jews saw the return to the land of Israel as a fulfillment of biblical prophecy. They believed that reclaiming the Promised Land was part of their divine destiny.

Bible: "I will bring them back to the land I gave to their ancestors, and they will take possession of it." (Jeremiah 30:3)

Quran: "And We said to the Children of Israel after Pharaoh, 'Dwell in the land, and when the [final] promise comes to pass, We will bring you forth as a gathering.'" (Quran 17:104)

Anti-Zionist Jewish Communities:

Some Orthodox Jews opposed Zionism, arguing that only the Messiah could lead them back to the Holy Land. This ideological divide highlighted the complexity within the Jewish diaspora itself.

Early Interactions with Palestinian Arabs

As Jewish immigrants began settling in Palestine, their interactions with the Arab population were initially peaceful but later became fraught with tension.

Land Purchases and Displacement:

Jewish immigrants often purchased land from absentee Arab landlords, leading to the displacement of Palestinian tenant farmers. This created resentment among the local population, as they saw their livelihoods threatened.

Zionist leaders emphasized the need for economic self-reliance, prioritizing Jewish labor on newly acquired lands, which further marginalized Arab workers.

Cultural and Social Exchanges:

In the early years, there were instances of cooperation, particularly in trade and agriculture, between Jewish settlers and Palestinian Arabs. However, as the influx of immigrants increased, the sense of competition and fear of losing cultural identity deepened.

Emerging Tensions:

Arab leaders began expressing concern over the growing Jewish presence, which they perceived as a potential threat to their sovereignty. This marked the beginning of a more organized resistance to Zionist aspirations.

The Role of Global Powers

The migration to Palestine did not occur in isolation; it was influenced and facilitated by major global powers.

The Ottoman Empire:

Initially tolerant, the Ottoman authorities grew wary of Zionist activities. They imposed restrictions on Jewish immigration and land purchases, fearing political unrest.

Despite these measures, Jewish organizations found ways to bypass these restrictions, often using intermediaries to acquire land.

The British Mandate:

The Balfour Declaration (1917) formalized British support for a Jewish homeland in Palestine. While it gave hope to Zionists, it also sowed the seeds of conflict by disregarding Arab opposition.

The British, tasked with administering Palestine after World War I, struggled to balance conflicting promises to Jews and Arabs, leading to increasing tensions.

Social and Economic Transformations in Palestine

The arrival of Jewish immigrants brought significant changes to Palestine's economy and society:

Agricultural Development:

Jewish settlers introduced modern agricultural techniques, transforming previously uncultivated land into productive farms.

The establishment of kibbutzim (collective farms) became a symbol of Zionist self-reliance and communal living.

Economic Inequality:

The economic success of Jewish settlements created disparities between the Jewish and Arab populations, exacerbating tensions. Palestinian Arabs, who lacked similar resources and international support, began to feel increasingly marginalized.

The Birth of Zionism

The rise of Zionism in the late 19th century was a direct response to these hardships. Zionism, led by figures like Theodor Herzl, advocated for the establishment of a Jewish homeland where Jews could live free from persecution.

Theodor Herzl and "The Jewish State" (1896):

Herzl, an Austro-Hungarian journalist, published Der Judenstaat (The Jewish State), arguing that Jews needed their own nation to escape the endless cycle of persecution. His vision gained widespread support, especially among Eastern European Jews.

The First Zionist Congress (1897):

Held in Basel, Switzerland, the congress formalized the Zionist movement. The delegates agreed that Palestine, the biblical homeland of the Jewish people, was the ideal location for this new state.

Early Migration to Palestine (Aliyah)

The migration of Jews to Palestine is often referred to as "Aliyah," meaning "ascent" in Hebrew. The late 19th and early 20th centuries saw several waves of Aliyah:

The First Aliyah (1882–1903):

Driven by pogroms and economic hardships in Eastern Europe, around 25,000 Jews migrated to Ottoman-controlled Palestine. They established agricultural settlements, such as Rishon LeZion and Petah Tikva, and revived Hebrew as a spoken language.

The Second Aliyah (1904–1914):

This wave brought approximately 35,000 Jews, many of whom were inspired by socialist ideals. They founded collective communities known as kibbutzim, which became a cornerstone of Israeli society.

The Role of the Ottoman Empire

At the time of these migrations, Palestine was part of the Ottoman Empire. The Ottomans initially allowed small numbers of Jewish immigrants to settle but grew increasingly wary as Zionist activity intensified.

Restrictions on Land Purchases:

In 1884, the Ottomans began restricting land sales to Jews. Despite these measures, Jewish organizations found ways to acquire land through intermediaries.

Jewish-Arab Relations:

Early interactions between Jewish settlers and Palestinian Arabs were generally peaceful. However, tensions began to rise as more Jews arrived and acquired land, often displacing Palestinian tenant farmers.

The Balfour Declaration and British Mandate

World War I marked a turning point in the Jewish migration to Palestine. In 1917, the British government issued the Balfour Declaration, pledging support for the establishment of a "national home for the Jewish people" in Palestine.

The Balfour Declaration (1917):

This declaration was seen as a major victory for the Zionist movement. However, it also sowed the seeds of conflict by disregarding the aspirations of the Palestinian Arab population.

The British Mandate (1920–1948):

After World War I, Britain took control of Palestine under a League of Nations mandate. During this period, Jewish immigration increased significantly, despite British attempts to limit it in response to Arab opposition.

The Holocaust and Mass Migration

The Holocaust during World War II was a cataclysmic event that solidified the urgency of a Jewish homeland.

The Exodus from Europe:

With six million Jews murdered by the Nazis, the survivors were left displaced and stateless. Many sought refuge in Palestine, often in defiance of British immigration restrictions.

The Ship "Exodus" (1947):

The plight of Holocaust survivors attempting to reach Palestine was epitomized by the ship Exodus, which carried over 4,500 Jewish refugees. The British intercepted the ship and sent its passengers back to Europe, sparking international outrage.

The Road to Statehood

By the mid-20th century, the Jewish population in Palestine had grown significantly, and the push for statehood gained momentum.

The UN Partition Plan (1947):

The United Nations proposed dividing Palestine into separate Jewish and Arab states, with Jerusalem under international control. The Jewish leadership accepted the plan, but the Arab states rejected it.

The Declaration of the State of Israel (1948):

On May 14, 1948, David Ben-Gurion declared the establishment of the State of Israel. This event marked the culmination of decades of migration and struggle but also ignited the first Arab-Israeli war.

Conclusion

The early migration of Jews to Palestine was driven by both desperation and aspiration, fueled by centuries of persecution and a longing for self-determination. However, the transformation of Palestine under Zionist initiatives, while remarkable, also sowed the seeds of conflict. The displacement of Palestinian Arabs and the growing tensions between the two communities highlighted the challenges of reconciling competing national identities—a challenge that continues to shape the region's history.

Chapter 4: The Zionist Movement and the Seeds of Modern Conflict

The migration of Jewish communities to Palestine during the late 19th and early 20th centuries set the stage for the Zionist movement. While earlier migrations were largely individual and religiously motivated, the rise of Zionism transformed this migration into an organized, political effort. This chapter explores the evolution of Zionism, its global support, and its impact on the socio-political landscape of Palestine, culminating in the initial seeds of modern conflict.

The Birth of Modern Zionism

Modern Zionism emerged from the struggles of Jewish communities in Europe. Facing centuries of persecution and exclusion, the Jewish people sought solutions to their existential challenges.

Theodor Herzl and the First Zionist Congress:

In 1897, Herzl convened the First Zionist Congress in Basel, Switzerland, formalizing the movement for a Jewish homeland. He emphasized the necessity of securing international support and organized Jewish migration to Palestine.

Nationalism and Jewish Identity:

Inspired by the wave of nationalism across Europe, Zionists envisioned a sovereign state for Jews to escape persecution and revive their cultural identity.

Early Migration and Settlement Strategies

Zionist efforts began to materialize through systematic migration to Palestine:

Aliyah Movements:

Beginning with the First Aliyah (1882–1903) and followed by subsequent waves, Zionists focused on agricultural settlements and rebuilding a Jewish presence in Palestine.

Land Purchases and Development:

Land was acquired primarily from absentee Arab landlords. Zionist organizations, such as the Jewish National Fund, facilitated these purchases, often displacing Palestinian tenants.

Kibbutzim and Collective Living:

The establishment of communal agricultural settlements (kibbutzim) became a cornerstone of Zionist philosophy, symbolizing self-reliance and unity.

The Balfour Declaration and British Mandate

Global political dynamics further advanced the Zionist agenda:

The Balfour Declaration (1917):

The British government declared its support for "the establishment in Palestine of a national home for the Jewish people." This document became a cornerstone of Zionist legitimacy but sparked fierce opposition among Palestinian Arabs.

The British Mandate:

Under the League of Nations mandate, Britain controlled Palestine, facilitating Jewish migration while attempting to manage growing tensions.

Rising Arab Opposition

As Jewish migration intensified, Palestinian Arabs began organizing resistance:

The Great Arab Revolt (1936–1939):

Fueled by grievances over British policies and land losses, Palestinians revolted against British rule and Zionist expansion.

Formation of National Identity:

Palestinian Arabs coalesced around their shared resistance, giving rise to a stronger sense of national identity.

Seeds of Conflict

The growing demographic and economic changes led to irreconcilable differences between Jews and Arabs:

Economic Displacement:

Zionist development often excluded Palestinians, creating resentment over lost land and opportunities.

Cultural Tensions:

The influx of European Jews brought cultural changes that clashed with the established traditions of Palestinian society.

Political Aspirations:

Both communities laid claim to Palestine, setting the stage for a contest over sovereignty.

Conclusion

By the 1940s, the foundations of the modern Israeli-Palestinian conflict had been laid. The Zionist movement, fueled by European nationalism and global political support, established a strong Jewish presence in Palestine. However, this progress came at the cost of growing tensions with the Arab population, whose land, identity, and aspirations were increasingly threatened.

Chapter 5: Partition, Independence, and the Nakba: The Birth of Israel and the Palestinian Catastrophe

The United Nations Partition Plan (1947)

In 1947, the United Nations proposed a plan to resolve the growing tensions in Palestine. Known as UN Resolution 181, the plan recommended dividing Palestine into two independent states: one Jewish and one Arab, with Jerusalem under international administration.

Jewish Acceptance:

The Jewish community, represented by the Zionist leadership, accepted the plan, viewing it as a pathway to achieving a sovereign state despite limitations on territory.

Arab Rejection:

Palestinian Arabs and surrounding Arab nations rejected the plan, arguing it was unjust to allocate over half of the land to a minority population. They also opposed the division of Jerusalem.

This disagreement set the stage for violence and deeper political rifts.

The Declaration of the State of Israel (1948)

On May 14, 1948, David Ben-Gurion, head of the Jewish Agency, declared the establishment of the State of Israel. This marked the culmination of decades of Zionist efforts.

Global Recognition:

The United States and the Soviet Union were among the first nations to recognize Israel, signaling early Cold War rivalries over influence in the Middle East.

Arab Response:

The declaration was met with outrage across the Arab world, leading to immediate military action by neighboring Arab states.

The First Arab-Israeli War (1948)

The day after Israel declared independence, five Arab nations (Egypt, Jordan, Syria, Lebanon, and Iraq) launched a military invasion to support Palestinian Arabs.

Israel's Military Advantage:

Despite being outnumbered, Israel's well-organized militias, such as the Haganah, and international support enabled it to repel the Arab forces.

Territorial Gains:

By the end of the war in 1949, Israel had expanded its territory beyond the UN partition plan, occupying about 78% of historic Palestine.

The Nakba (1948)

For Palestinians, 1948 marks the Nakba, or "Catastrophe," a term that encapsulates the loss of land, displacement, and the destruction of their society.

Mass Displacement:

Over 700,000 Palestinians were forced to flee or were expelled from their homes. Many sought refuge in neighboring countries, including Jordan, Lebanon, and Syria, where they lived in overcrowded refugee camps.

Destroyed Villages:

Approximately 500 Palestinian villages were depopulated or destroyed, erasing centuries of history and culture.

Denial of Return:

Despite UN resolutions calling for the right of Palestinian refugees to return, Israel consistently refused, citing security concerns and the demographic threat to the Jewish state.

The Armistice Agreements (1949)

By 1949, ceasefire agreements were brokered under UN supervision, resulting in:

Division of Territory:

Israel controlled the majority of the land.

Jordan annexed the West Bank, including East Jerusalem.

Egypt administered the Gaza Strip.

No Resolution for Refugees:

The agreements did not address the status of Palestinian refugees, laying the groundwork for future conflict.

The Impact of the Nakba and the Creation of Israel

For Israel:

The creation of a sovereign state fulfilled Zionist aspirations.

However, it also marked the beginning of perpetual hostility with neighboring Arab countries and Palestinian resistance.

For Palestinians:

The Nakba remains a central trauma, symbolizing loss, dispossession, and ongoing struggle.

Palestinian identity solidified around the collective memory of the catastrophe and the hope for justice.

Conclusion

The events of 1948 reshaped the Middle East and the global political landscape. The creation of Israel and the Palestinian Nakba remain deeply intertwined, serving as the foundation for decades of conflict and unrest. The next chapter will explore the subsequent wars, including the Six-Day War, and their role in shaping the modern boundaries and tensions of the region.

Chapter 6: Wars, Occupations, and the Expansion of Boundaries

The Suez Crisis (1956)

In 1956, tensions between Israel and Egypt escalated over the nationalization of the Suez Canal by Egyptian President Gamal Abdel Nasser. In response, Israel joined forces with Britain and France in a coordinated military assault on Egypt.

The Operation:

Israel invaded the Sinai Peninsula, swiftly defeating Egyptian forces and securing strategic points. Britain and France intervened under the pretext of separating the warring sides but aimed to regain control of the Suez Canal.

International Response:

The crisis attracted global condemnation. Under pressure from the United States and the Soviet Union, the invading forces withdrew. This event marked the emergence of the United States as a dominant power in Middle Eastern affairs.

Outcome for Israel:

The Suez Crisis solidified Israel's military confidence and secured temporary navigation rights in the Straits of Tiran, essential for trade and security.

The Six-Day War (1967)

The Six-Day War, fought from June 5 to June 10, 1967, was a transformative conflict that reshaped the region.

Pre-War Tensions:

Escalating hostilities included Egypt's blockade of Israeli shipping routes and troop mobilization in the Sinai. Syria, Jordan, and Iraq also joined in threatening Israel.

The War:

Israel launched preemptive air strikes, crippling Arab air forces. Within six days, Israel captured:

The West Bank and East Jerusalem from Jordan.

The Gaza Strip and Sinai Peninsula from Egypt.

The Golan Heights from Syria.

Consequences:

Israel tripled its territory, achieving strategic depth but igniting international criticism for occupying Arab lands.

The war led to the displacement of over 300,000 Palestinians.

United Nations Security Council Resolution 242 called for Israel's withdrawal from occupied territories, which remains a cornerstone of peace negotiations.

The Yom Kippur War (1973)

On October 6, 1973, during the Jewish holy day of Yom Kippur, Egypt and Syria launched a surprise attack on Israel to reclaim lost territories.

Early Arab Success:

Egyptian forces crossed the Suez Canal and overwhelmed Israeli defenses, while Syrian troops advanced in the Golan Heights.

Israel's Counteroffensive:

After initial losses, Israel, with significant U.S. support, regrouped and pushed Arab forces back. By the war's end, Israeli forces were close to Cairo and Damascus.

Impact:

The war demonstrated Arab nations' determination to challenge Israel.

It led to increased U.S. involvement in the Middle East, as well as the eventual Camp David Accords between Egypt and Israel.

The Beginning of Israeli Settlements

Following the Six-Day War, Israel began constructing settlements in the West Bank, Gaza Strip, and East Jerusalem.

Motivations:

Religious Zionists saw the occupied territories as part of the biblical "Land of Israel."

Politically, settlements were a way to establish facts on the ground and deter Palestinian statehood.

Consequences:

Settlements became a major obstacle to peace, with the international community deeming them illegal under international law.

They exacerbated tensions and contributed to frequent violence.

Palestinian Resistance and the PLO

The rise of the Palestinian Liberation Organization (PLO) in the 1960s marked a new phase of resistance.

Formation of the PLO:

Established in 1964, the PLO aimed to liberate Palestine through armed struggle.

Yasser Arafat's leadership in 1969 made the PLO a unifying force for Palestinians worldwide.

Acts of Resistance:

The PLO orchestrated guerrilla attacks, including cross-border raids and hijackings, targeting Israeli interests globally.

Israeli Retaliation:

Israel responded with military operations against PLO bases in neighboring countries, including Lebanon and Jordan.

Global Dynamics and the Arab-Israeli Conflict

The Arab-Israeli wars drew the involvement of global powers:

The United States emerged as Israel's primary ally, providing economic aid and military support.

The Soviet Union backed Arab states, deepening Cold War rivalries in the Middle East.

These alignments shaped regional politics, with both superpowers using the conflict to assert influence.

Conclusion

The wars and occupations of the 20th century defined the modern Israeli-Palestinian conflict. Israel's territorial expansion and the resulting Palestinian displacement deepened animosities, while the rise of settlements and armed resistance further entrenched divisions.

The next chapter will delve into the intifadas (uprisings) and the quest for peace, examining how grassroots movements and diplomatic efforts have sought to resolve one of history's most enduring conflicts.

Chapter 7: Intifada and the Struggle for Peace

The Israeli-Palestinian conflict, deeply rooted in history, saw significant escalations during the late 20th and early 21st centuries. The uprisings, or intifadas, marked turning points in the struggle, with widespread grassroots resistance against Israeli occupation. This chapter delves into the causes, dynamics, and impacts of the two major intifadas and examines the peace processes that sought to resolve the conflict amidst entrenched divisions.

The First Intifada (1987–1993): A Grassroots Uprising

Background and Causes

The First Intifada erupted in December 1987 in the Jabalia refugee camp in Gaza, following a traffic incident where an Israeli truck killed four Palestinians. This seemingly ordinary event ignited widespread anger that had been simmering due to years of military occupation, land seizures, economic hardships, and political frustration.

Key contributing factors included:

Economic Deprivation: Palestinian workers in the occupied territories faced discrimination and lacked access to economic opportunities.

Land Appropriation: The expansion of Israeli settlements in the West Bank and Gaza intensified grievances.

Political Stalemate: The lack of progress towards Palestinian self-determination underlined growing resentment.

Forms of Resistance

The First Intifada was characterized by non-violent and violent forms of resistance:

Civil Disobedience: Strikes, boycotts of Israeli goods, refusal to pay taxes, and protests were widespread.

Youth-Led Resistance: Palestinian youths, armed with rocks and makeshift weapons, became symbols of defiance against Israeli forces.

Grassroots Organization: Local committees coordinated activities, marking a shift from reliance on the Palestine Liberation Organization (PLO) abroad to internal leadership.

Israeli Response

Israel deployed heavy-handed measures to suppress the uprising, including curfews, mass arrests, and demolitions of Palestinian homes. The conflict resulted in significant casualties, with over 1,000 Palestinians killed and thousands more injured by the end of the Intifada.

Impact

Global Attention: The Intifada brought international focus to the Palestinian struggle, forcing the Israeli-Palestinian conflict into global discourse.

Rise of Hamas: Amid the uprising, the Islamic Resistance Movement (Hamas) emerged as a political and militant force, challenging the PLO's dominance.

The Oslo Accords: A Glimmer of Hope (1993)

Negotiations and Agreement

The First Intifada created momentum for peace talks, culminating in the Oslo Accords signed in 1993. Negotiated in secret, the agreement was brokered by Norwegian diplomats and marked a historic turning point:

Mutual Recognition: The PLO recognized Israel's right to exist, and Israel acknowledged the PLO as the representative of the Palestinian people.

Framework for Peace: The accords outlined the creation of a Palestinian Authority (PA) to govern parts of the West Bank and Gaza. Further negotiations were planned for final-status issues, including refugees, Jerusalem, and borders.

Challenges and Criticism

While Oslo generated optimism, it also faced significant criticism:

Ambiguity: The accords left key issues unresolved, leading to disillusionment on both sides.

Opposition: Hardline factions in both Israel and Palestine opposed the agreements. Israeli settlers and Palestinian militant groups, such as Hamas, viewed the accords as a betrayal of their respective causes.

The Second Intifada (2000–2005): Escalation of Violence

Trigger and Outbreak

The Second Intifada, or Al-Aqsa Intifada, erupted in September 2000 after Israeli opposition leader Ariel Sharon visited the Al-Aqsa Mosque compound in Jerusalem. The visit was perceived as a provocation, sparking widespread protests that quickly escalated into violent clashes.

Key Features

Unlike the First Intifada, the Second Intifada was marked by widespread use of arms and explosive devices.

Suicide Bombings: Hamas and other militant groups launched numerous suicide attacks targeting Israeli civilians.

Israeli Military Campaigns: Israel responded with major military offensives, including Operation Defensive Shield, which reoccupied Palestinian cities and refugee camps.

Construction of the Separation Barrier: To prevent attacks, Israel began building a barrier in the West Bank, which Palestinians viewed as a land grab.

Casualties and Destruction

The Second Intifada was far more deadly than the first:

Over 3,000 Palestinians and 1,000 Israelis were killed.

Infrastructure in Palestinian territories was severely damaged, exacerbating economic and humanitarian crises

Political Consequences

Weakening of the PA: Israel marginalized the Palestinian Authority, accusing its leader, Yasser Arafat, of supporting violence.

Rise of Militancy: Groups like Hamas and Islamic Jihad gained prominence, further dividing Palestinian leadership.

The Struggle for Peace: Post-Intifada Efforts

The Roadmap to Peace (2003)

A peace plan introduced by the United States, European Union, United Nations, and Russia proposed a phased approach towards a two-state solution.

Goals: The establishment of a Palestinian state alongside Israel by 2005.

Challenges: Continued violence and mutual distrust derailed progress.

The Gaza Disengagement (2005)

Israel, under Prime Minister Ariel Sharon, unilaterally withdrew from Gaza, dismantling settlements and military presence.

Palestinian Control: The move handed Gaza to Palestinian authority but also led to increased internal division, as Hamas took control of Gaza in 2007 following elections and clashes with the PA.

Ongoing Challenges

Despite these efforts, peace remains elusive due to:

Settlement Expansion: Continued Israeli settlement activity undermines the feasibility of a two-state solution.

Internal Divisions: The split between Fatah (in the West Bank) and Hamas (in Gaza) weakens the Palestinian position in negotiations.

Regional Instability: Geopolitical tensions in the Middle East complicate resolution efforts.

Conclusion

The intifadas and subsequent peace efforts highlight the deep-rooted complexities of the Israeli-Palestinian conflict. While the uprisings showcased Palestinian resistance and aspirations for statehood, the cycles of violence and failed negotiations have entrenched divisions further. The road to peace requires addressing historical grievances, ensuring justice, and fostering mutual trust—an immense but essential challenge for both nations and the global community.

Chapter 8: Justice Through Law – The Only Solution

The Israeli-Palestinian conflict has persisted for decades, fueled by historical grievances, religious undertones, and geopolitical interests. However, a resolution cannot rest on the basis of religion, power, or propaganda. The only sustainable solution lies in adherence to international law, ensuring justice, equity, and the protection of human rights. This chapter explores the transformation of Palestine, the role of global media, and the urgent need for fairness to address the plight of the Palestinian people.

The Principle of Justice Through Law

The Role of International Law:

The world has established laws to protect nations and individuals from aggression, displacement, and discrimination. Core principles of the United Nations Charter and international conventions stress:

Sovereignty: Every nation has the right to exist and govern its territory.

Human Rights: Every individual has the right to live in peace, dignity, and security, irrespective of religion or ethnicity.

The Illegality of Occupation: The annexation of territories through force or settlement contravenes international law, such as the Geneva Conventions.

Failure to Uphold Justice:

Despite these principles, the case of Palestine remains an open wound in international relations:

Israel's occupation of the West Bank, Gaza Strip, and East Jerusalem violates multiple UN resolutions, including Resolution 242, which calls for withdrawal from occupied territories.

Palestinians continue to face home demolitions, land confiscation, and restricted mobility, violating their basic rights under international law.

Beyond Religion – A Case of Justice:

This conflict must not be reduced to a religious or cultural struggle between Jews and Muslims. It is fundamentally about justice for a displaced people.

The narrative of justice emphasizes the rights of Palestinians to reclaim their land and live without oppression.

Ensuring justice for Palestine sets a precedent for protecting oppressed communities worldwide.

The Changing Map of Palestine

Palestine Before 1948:

Historically, Palestine was home to a diverse population of Muslims, Christians, and Jews living under Ottoman and British rule.

Before the establishment of Israel, the majority of the population was Palestinian Arab, and Jewish communities coexisted as minorities.

UN Partition Plan (1947):

The United Nations proposed dividing Palestine into two states—one Jewish and one Arab. The Jewish community accepted the plan, but the Arab population rejected it, viewing it as unjust.

Under this plan, 55% of the land was allocated to the Jewish state, despite Jews comprising only 33% of the population.

Post-1948 Nakba:

The 1948 Arab-Israeli War resulted in the displacement of over 700,000 Palestinians and the destruction of hundreds of villages. By the war's end, Israel controlled 78% of historical Palestine, far exceeding the partition plan.

Post-1967 and Modern-Day Map:

Following the Six-Day War (1967), Israel occupied the West Bank, Gaza Strip, and East Jerusalem.

Today, the map of Palestine has been reduced to fragmented enclaves in the West Bank and Gaza, surrounded by Israeli-controlled areas.

The Separation Wall and expanding Israeli settlements have further divided Palestinian territories, making a contiguous Palestinian state nearly impossible.

A Visual Erasure of Palestine:

The changing map is not just about territory but about identity. Palestinian towns and villages have been renamed or replaced by Israeli settlements, erasing centuries of history and culture.

The Role of Media in Shaping Narratives

Global Silence and Propaganda:

Media coverage plays a significant role in shaping public opinion about the Israeli-Palestinian conflict. However, the narrative has often been skewed or suppressed.

Silence: Many mainstream media outlets in Western nations avoid criticizing Israeli policies due to political pressures and fear of being labeled anti-Semitic.

Propaganda: In some cases, media frames Palestinians as aggressors, ignoring their decades of suffering under occupation.

For instance, resistance movements are often labeled as "terrorist organizations" without context about the oppression they face.

Selective Reporting:

Palestinian voices and stories of suffering—displacement, killings, and apartheid-like conditions—are frequently underreported or dismissed.

Coverage of violence often centers on Israeli casualties while downplaying the disproportionate number of Palestinian victims.

The Role of Social Media:

Social media has become a platform for Palestinians to share their stories directly with the world.

However, many platforms are accused of censorship, removing Palestinian content under vague policies.

The Danger of Biased Narratives:

Skewed media portrayals fuel misconceptions, delay justice, and embolden aggressors.

A balanced narrative must emphasize the humanitarian crisis faced by Palestinians, shedding light on their status as victims of occupation and displacement.

Displacement and Statelessness:

Palestinians remain one of the largest stateless populations in the world, with millions living as refugees in neighboring countries.

Over 5 million registered Palestinian refugees live in camps, many in abject poverty.

Israel's refusal to allow their return contravenes UN Resolution 194, which affirms the right of Palestinian refugees to return to their homes.

Humanitarian Crisis:

Gaza, under an Israeli blockade since 2007, faces severe shortages of food, medicine, and electricity. The region is often described as an "open-air prison."

In the West Bank, Palestinians endure checkpoints, military raids, and land confiscation.

The Erasure of Identity:

The loss of land, destruction of homes, and suppression of cultural heritage symbolize an attempt to erase Palestinian identity.

Conclusion

The ongoing conflict between Israel and Palestine is not just a political issue; it is a moral one. The world must rise above propaganda, political interests, and religious biases to address this crisis through the lens of justice and international law.

Key Takeaways:

The Palestinians are victims of historical injustices, displacement, and continued oppression.

Justice requires the global community to enforce international law without bias, ensuring the rights of Palestinians to their land, freedom, and dignity.

Media must play a responsible role in amplifying the truth and holding perpetrators accountable.

Ultimately, the Palestinian struggle is a fight for basic human rights and justice. Recognizing them as victims is the first step toward finding a just and lasting solution to one of the most enduring conflicts of modern times.

Conclusion

The story of Israel and Palestine is a profound and complex narrative that reflects humanity's struggles with faith, identity, and justice. This book has aimed to provide a comprehensive understanding of the historical roots and contemporary challenges of this enduring conflict, emphasizing the critical role of justice and international law as the foundation for peace.

The resolution of this conflict is not a matter of choosing sides based on religion or politics but a commitment to fairness and humanity. Only by recognizing the rights and dignity of all people involved can we hope to achieve lasting peace. It is our responsibility to advocate for those who have been silenced and displaced, to ensure that justice prevails for the oppressed.

May this book serve as a reminder of the importance of truth, dialogue, and empathy in addressing one of the most significant moral challenges of our time.

Acknowledgments

This book would not have been possible without the contributions, guidance, and support of many individuals and communities.

I extend my deepest gratitude to scholars, researchers, and advocates who have tirelessly documented the realities of the Israeli-Palestinian conflict. Your dedication to uncovering the truth and promoting justice has been instrumental in shaping the ideas and narratives in this work.

To my family and friends, thank you for your unwavering encouragement and belief in this project. Your support has been a source of strength throughout this journey

To the readers, I am profoundly grateful for your time and attention. Your willingness to engage with this complex subject reflects a commitment to understanding and action. May this book inspire you to advocate for justice and peace in all its forms.

Finally, to all those who have suffered and continue to struggle in the face of oppression, know that your resilience is a beacon of hope. The pursuit of justice and peace must remain steadfast, guided by compassion and fairness for all.

Thank you.

Also by Dans Hardyans

The Kopi Luwak Legacy: Tradition, Taste and Truth
Unveiling The Veil Two Nation: Israel and Palestine

www.ingramcontent.com/pod-product-compliance
Lightning Source LLC
LaVergne TN
LVHW091230150826
845673LV00003B/1080
9798230058465